CONTENTS

ATHEISM

Atheism:

RMPS Advanced

Higher

Laura Crichton

Edited by Gavin Park

ISBN: 9781076924926

DEDICATION

To my Advanced Higher pupils – both past and future...

1 THE RISE OF ATHEISM

Is God willing to prevent evil, but not able?

Then he is not omnipotent.

Is he able, but not willing?

Then he is malevolent.

Is he both able, and willing?

Then whence cometh evil?

Is he neither willing, nor able?

Then why call him God?"

- Epicurus

Typically thought of as one of the first arguments for Atheism, one could be forgiven for thinking the rise of Atheism seen in today's society is nothing new. However a brief examination of the centuries that have followed Epicurus will show that time, misunderstanding and indeed, malice have distorted many of the writers of the past.

One first must consider the time Epicurus was writing in, the Greek understanding of God was far from the Judeo-Christian ideas held in the West today. It is unlikely that he even said 'God' (if he truly said this at all) given that Greek society was based on a belief in a variety of gods - none of which possessed the supernatural attributes with which we are familiar. For the Ancient Greeks the gods of Olympia were immoral humans with no restraint, they were egocentric, jealous and petty tyrants with limited spheres of influence e.g. Poseidon - the god of the sea or Demeter - the goddess of harvest and fertility. In 444BC when setting up the governing laws of the new city-state of Thurioi, Protagorus insisted on public accountability – not like the gods of Olympus.

It is at this time the term 'atheistos' emerges but not with the meaning we may imagine; roughly translated it means 'one who denies the traditional religion of the Athenian establishment.' No one was denying the existence of a deity at this point; rather they were questioning the scope of the gods' powers. Although as we see with the death of Socrates in 399BC - who was sentenced to death for corrupting the youth of Athens by introducing strange gods - this was considered to be a serious offence the Ancient Greeks. But they were not brandishing quite the same arguments as we see from atheist authors today.

Conversely the first Christians were also called atheists for denial of the traditional Roman gods. So perhaps the atheism found in ancient history is best described as 'disbelief in the state religion of the time.'

Obviously Christianity did not sink into oblivion, and with some militant support and the formation of the Church, became firmly embedded in Europe. It is not until the 15th century that we really find cracks beginning to appear in the stronghold of Christendom.

The 15th century saw a variety of Christian Reformation: Luther, Zwingli, Calvin and others railed against the Church with ideas; Francis I took military action, whilst Henry VIII simply denied the authority of the church and took over as supreme head in England. Whilst none of these Reformers challenged the idea of God they did begin to attack the ideas on which the church was based. This proved to be a popular notion, however, at times it is difficult to tell whether arguments denoted as 'atheist' are really attacks on God or the church.

Given that religion is really the term given to a set of recognised beliefs, and the church is a product of religion, perhaps it is not that surprising. However when writers rage against individual religious institutions, it gives rise to the question whether any good arguments for atheism are actually liable to emerge from it.

Into the 17th century Atheism did not make much of headway in Britain; in 1689 the Act of Toleration was signed allowing diversity of belief rather than a state dictated religion. Although criticism of Christianity continued, faith in a God did not truly erode. Even in the 18th century, David Hume, thought of as a major influence in the rise of atheism, commented that he had never actually met an atheist. This is not to say Hume had no social life but rather there was a distinct lack of people in Britain who were willing to define themselves in this way.

This was not the case across Europe. 1789 saw the start French Revolution; the Church had supported the monarchy and was seen as a suppressing development. To eliminate God was to allow a new future to dawn. Once again the question arises as to whether these ideas were truly disbelief in God or disbelief in the Church.

Writers from this time such as Meslier, Diderot, Rousseau and Voltaire have all been held up as stalwarts of Atheism - however arguably they would be better described as deists. They believed that Church was corrupt, that it was built on lies but that it had simply distorted the truth of God. They did not reject the supernatural but rather the theology of the church.

Modern writers have a slight tendency to exaggerate the historicity and impact of atheism to further their case and we see this particularly in the case of Voltaire, who is often cited by atheist apologists to say 'If God did not exist, it would be necessary to invent Him.' Missing out the next sentence 'Who the sage proclaims, and whom kings adore.' Voltaire defended the notion of a supreme being he just believed it to be hijacked by the World's religions.

That is not to say that the Revolution was devoid of Atheist ideas. La Mettrie, Helvetices and particularly d'Holbach put forward ideas that ignorance gives birth to God and that progress could only be made if society turned to reason and experience. It is at this point we really see God explained away as an infantile idea and reason for disbelief in the divine rather than the church emerging. Whilst d'Holbach made atheism credible; the Marquis de Sade made it interesting – within his writing he put forth the idea that by abandoning God we could truly be happy. Without the restraint of divine moral we could truly embrace life – in his case embarking on a notorious life of sexual sadism!

By 1799, politicians and the power hungry had killed the Revolution and a new constitution proclaimed 'Citizens, the Revolution is established upon the principle which began it: it is over." The restoration of Catholicism soon followed, however not all the ideas died away.

The 19th century saw the emergence of Feuerbach, Marx and Freud who saw God as merely an invention. Feuerbach put forward the idea that if the church's basic ideas were proven to be flawed, then social authority would be reduced. He set out to demonstrate that the idea of God was merely a consolation of sorrow in life and that the world was being suppressed by its own invention. Marx too, proposed that religion arose from social situations; it was an opiate to suppress the poor, an ill cured by social reform. For Freud, God was the invention of the human unconscious. It is perhaps important to note at this stage, that for each of these writers, atheism did not emerge as a result of there findings but was a presupposition – an a priori claim if you will – obviously limiting the power of their argumentation.

However, the powerful criticism of religious belief initiated by Feuerbach and developed by Marx and Freud has had a formative impact on twentieth-century Western culture. The credibility of these criticisms rested on the widespread belief that they were fundamentally scientific in character – in other words, that the origins of religious belief could be explained in terms of socioeconomic factors of human psychology in just the same way as physics explained the movement of the planets. Belief in God was widely seen as a construct of the consolation-seeking human mind, which would evaporate with further scientific advance. It's interesting to note however, that this isn't actually attacking the concept of God but rather belief itself.

Moving into the 20th century we see the emergence the now embedded idea of Science standing in opposition of Religion. The 1870's saw the publication of John Draper's History of the Conflict between Religion and Science and Andrew Dickson White's History of Warfare of Science with Theology in Christendom and most notably, William Clifford's Ethics of Belief in which he put forth an idea that would continue to resonate throughout the following centuries: 'It is wrong always, everywhere, and for anyone, to believe anything upon insufficient evidence.'

Atheist writers of the 19th century often defined their position in terms of absence – rather than a denial – of a belief in God and argued that the burden of proof lay with those who had faith. Unsurprisingly perhaps, in 1869, Thomas Huxley introduced the term 'agnostic' proposing that 'it is impossible to arrive at any degree of meta-physical certainty in these matters.' This did little more than irritate both sides of the table, believing that Huxley was seemly dodging the question.

It is in this age that we see William Paley's watch analogy from 1802 gaining recognition: throughout the 19th century undergraduates at Cambridge were required to read it, indeed, his ideas were largely accepted by natural scientists in the first half of the 19th century; Darwin, himself an undergraduate at Cambridge commented 'I was charmed and convinced of the long line of argumentation.' However, as we now know Darwin discovery of natural selection has a devastating affect on Paley's argument. Indeed, Modern Atheists now herald Darwin's theory as the final nail in God's coffin! However it would be wrong to view Darwin as an atheist himself; certainly he viewed many religious doctrines such as original sin with distaste, as did many of his time, but he never did commit himself in either direction and perhaps can best be described as agnostic.

In order for Darwin's theory of Evolution to have significance to the debate over atheism, a concept of God must be proposed that is demonstrably in conflict with Darwin. In his haste to present a compelling argument for God, Paley certainly did this, proposing a designer to have created all things in their present form. However many theologians disagreed on this point proposing that God made things to make themselves; an idea can be viewed as in line with Darwin. This argument still pervades today with the 'warfare of science with theology' largely can be won or lost on interpretation and it is here that we find the debate today.

In the 21st century, we have seen the rise of 'New Atheism, a term applied, sometime pejoratively, to a series of six best-selling books that appeared from 2005-2006. Sam Harris, Daniel Dennett, Richard Dawkins, Victor Stenger and Christopher Hitchens are often cited to be the leaders of this movement. In essence there message is simple, Atheism just makes more sense. Highlighting recent scientific development, some time is spent debunking old theology such as Aquinas or Paley but this new movement goes much further than before. Targeting Christianity in particular, they do not just ridicule religion, saying it's a crutch or a drug, they believe that the time has come that religion should simply not be tolerated but should be countered, criticised and exposed by rational argument wherever its influence arises.

To some, the response of the Christian wing is fairly embarrassing. Fundamentally, the theologians have nothing new. The fact that we still teach the Cosmological and Teleological Arguments - which both have their roots in Ancient History - shows how little theology has really changed. Richard Dawkin's book, 'The Blind Watchmaker' is clearly a reference to Paley but one must question how many theists actually believe in God on the basis of the these arguments?

Many popular Atheist arguments still focus on the idea that religion is bad rather than debunking the concept of God. Once again, one can question the relevance of this debate - just because there are bad religious people does that prove God does not exist?

2 THE PRESUMPTION OF ATHEISM

Before entering into any real discussion of atheism, it is useful to consider what is understood by the terminology at hand. Atheism, most simply, is the position that God does not exist - in any form. There is nothing behind the universe as we observe it. There is no soul that exists beyond our bodies. No miracles or spiritual plain. And certainly no supernatural entity lurking above us ready to pass judgement. In many ways, it would be legitimate to describe atheists as naturalists, those who believe there is only the natural world. They do not deny consciousness, emotion or beauty; everything is just firmly in the natural realm.

Antony Flew (before his alleged conversion to Deism) wrote a paper entitled 'The Presumption of Atheism', in which he urged that we further categorise atheism into **positive atheism** and **negative atheism**. These are sometimes referred to as Strong and Weak Atheism respectively. In Flew's interpretation, a Positive

Atheist is defined as someone who positively asserts the non-existence of God; they believe that they are able to prove that God does not exist. Whereas a negative atheist is simply not a theist.

Agnosticism sits apart from atheism in that agnostics believe that it is impossible to know – at least at the present time – whether God exists or not, and so maintain that the only rational option is to reserve judgment. This is distinct from the negative atheist because they have not yet conceded that God is a legitimate concept; the negative atheist maintains that in the absence of evidence it is right to disbelieve. To understand why this is important it may be useful to consider Bertrand Russell's 'teapot analogy.' In an unpublished article entitled 'Is There a God?', Russell wrote:

> *If I were to suggest that between the Earth and Mars there is a china teapot revolving about the sun in an elliptical orbit, nobody would be able to disprove my assertion provided I were careful to add that the teapot is too small to be revealed even by our most powerful telescopes. But if I were to go on to say that, since my assertion cannot be disproved, it is intolerable presumption on the part of human reason*

to doubt it, I should rightly be thought to be talking nonsense. If, however, the existence of such a teapot were affirmed in ancient books, taught as the sacred truth every Sunday, and instilled into the minds of children at school, hesitation to believe in its existence would become a mark of eccentricity and entitle the doubter to the attentions of the psychiatrist in an enlightened age or of the Inquisitor in an earlier time.

There are four possible responses to this celestial teapot: assume it exists despite the lack of evidence (theism), reserve judgment in the absence of any evidence to prove or disprove its existence (agnosticism), apply logic and reason, highlight the lack of evidence for the teapot a this time, and presume that it does not exist (negative atheism), or investigate the concept fully and attempt to provide evidence of its non-existence (positive atheism).

Note – appreciate the difference between assumption and presumption. Assumptions are beliefs not support by reason or logic. Presumption is a form of belief that is support with reason and logic.

If the logic of agnosticism was applied in this scenario, you would have no choice but to be a teapot agnostic. It then follows that you would have to be agnostic about any issue on which there was possibility you could be wrong. In life there is no absolute certainty about anything. But in the scenario presented by Russell we would not hesitate to dismiss the idea of a celestial teapot; we would not view it as a legitimate concept. Given it's ridiculous nature, it is unlikely that many of us would go out of our way to prove that it wasn't there either. It is up to the 'teapotians' to show it is a legitimate concept; we must presume it does not exist until shown otherwise.

Presumption

Antony Flew wrote in his 1984 book, God, Freedom and Immorality: *"The onus of proof lies on the man who affirms, not on the man who denies."* Whilst one could argue that Positive Atheists are also 'affirming' something - in that they are positively asserting that God does not exist - Flew makes the point that they cannot do so until the proposition i.e. the theists have provided them with something to demolish.

Flew argued that the case for atheism should be addressed rather like any other in the UK legal system. In a court case the defendant is assumed innocent until proven guilty, or rather a position of neutrality is adopted. This indicates where the court starts and how it must proceed; the burden is on the prosecution to prove guilt. Where this is not possible, the benefit of the doubt is given to avoid punishing the innocent even if a few guilty people remain unpunished.

Flew said, like innocence, we should also presume negative atheism, at least until there were grounds or evidence for God's existence. From this starting point it should be noted that, you could find proof or disproof but by starting from a neutral standpoint you are less likely to start with a bias. Like the legal system there may well be some things that are true that we will not believe, but it is better to avoid believing in false things.

Against this, there are numerous events in life that not guaranteed, such as the belief that the sun will rise tomorrow, yet belief that it will is more than respectable. It is at this point that it perhaps useful to turn to inductivism.

Induction

An inductive argument is one in which the premises are supposed to support the conclusion in such a way that, if the premises are true, it is improbable that the conclusion would be false. Thus, the conclusion follows probably from the premises and inferences. Going back to our previous example, of the sun rising tomorrow, it is reasonable to infer and thus believe it will because it has every single day of our existence. It is a strong inductive argument. In the case of God, it is the place of the theist to find premises that support God's existence.

Many theists would argue that they do have proof. One may question whether God can really be compared to a celestial teapot: Theists argue that people have experienced God. Indeed, in his *Gifford Lectures,* William James explored the variety of religious experiences and hit on a number of points; religion has defined many moments of history and its effects can clearly be seen, whilst not always positive, lives have undoubtably be changed. There are also many similarities between the descriptions of religious experience, and indeed, there are many such testimonies from around the world. In short, people usually tell the truth and the number of people who have all ascribed to the same version of events, cannot easily be ignored. There is reason for belief in God.

Contrary to this, in his essay 'On Belief in Miracles' David Hume wrote, "The gazing populace receive greedily, without examination, whatever soothes superstition and promotes wonder." Hume argued that human beings have a natural tendency to be bewitched by wonder and mystery which gives us a strong desire to believe in the extraordinary. It follows that whilst there may be some things that remain unexplained, atheists argue that by using inductive logic (using past experiences to make inferences about the future) then it is reasonable to suggest that the explanation will be naturalistic. In the past, humanity had thought that events could only be brought about by the supernatural (such as the creation of man) but experience has shown that this is not the case (evolution). It would unreasonable to presume that this would not continue to be the case.

One must always concede that inductive logic has its limitations. Inductive logic does not produce philosophical truths but rather probable conclusions because we cannot presume that premises based on experience will always remain the same i.e. there may one day find an event without a naturalistic explanation. However even though it may be shown to be wrong one day, but that does not mean that there is not good reason for adopting a position of disbelief in the meantime.

Abduction

However there is also another type of argument that is useful to the 'God' debate. Abduction is where a phenomenon that has more than one possible explanation and attempts are made to determine which of these explanations is best. Although abductive arguments draw on the inductive principle that the unobserved past, present and future resembles the observed past and present, they are structured differently. There is no magic formula for determining which explanation is the best, but in general better explanations are simpler, more coherent, and more comprehensive that the alternatives.

In the case of God, abduction is useful because there are many explanations for the way the world appears to be, since many conflict with each other they cannot all be true therefore we must find the one that fits best:

Option One: Classical Theism.

A form of monotheism where one believes in a God that is omniscient (all-knowing), omnipotent (all-powerful), omnibenevolent (completely good), and traditionally thought of

as both immanent (within the world) whilst simultaneously transcendent (beyond the universe.) He would also be deemed as infinite - without measure and timeless - as well playing a role in the creation of the universe.

Option Two: Deism

The idea that God did (or still) exists as the cause of the universe but has subsequently left or shows no interest in interacting with it. Others would define deism as believing in a god with flaws or reduced power, but still the need to have something beyond the natural world.

Option Three: Atheism

Be it positive or negative, weak or strong, the final position would be to reject the concept of God and focus on life in the natural world.

Whilst other options obviously exist, given the prior rejection of agnosticism these three seem to provide the most interest.

The God of Classical Theism is obviously the one described by all three of the major monotheistic religions - Judaism, Christianity, and Islam. Given that believers account for over 50% of the world's population - it's obviously a popular option but that doesn't mean it's right. The option of atheism - the explicit rejection of classical theism obviously also makes sense as an option. But why deism?

As the debate progresses and our understanding of 'God' changes it will be interesting to assess whether the God of traditional theism is logically possible. Or whether actually, only rational belief in deism is possible if one is to maintain belief in the supernatural. One could question whether there is any harm believing in God? But one only has to point to religious crusades and creationists to find an answer. One also has to question the wisdom of wantonly living in ignorance; humanity has always sought to further their knowledge, questioning and challenging existing ideas and theories in order to progress. So why stop now?

3 THE INCOHERENCE OF THE GOD OF CLASSICAL THEISM

Agnostics have been criticized by some atheists because they have conceded to the theist that God, considered in himself, is at least a possible being: even if He does not exist, He is the sort of being who could exist. Regardless of whether God's existence would be compatible with anything else, such as modern science or the existence of evil, there are some who argue that it is not even compatible with itself – this is often referred to as internal coherence. It follows that if the attributes of God can be successfully found to be self-contradictory then it would logically it is fair to say such a God would not exist.

Omnipotence

Revelation 19:6

Then I heard something like the voice of a great multitude and like the sound of many waters and like the sound of mighty peals of thunder, saying, "Hallelujah! For the Lord our God, the Almighty, reigns.

The term omnipotence stems from the Latin, *Omni Potens* best translated as 'all-powerful.' Resulting, one attributed with omnipotence is thought of as being able to do anything and everything. This seems relatively straightforward – to remain a logical concept, we must show that God can be anything. However even this one attribute throws up a number of problems – Can God draw a square triangle? Can He create a colourless orange ball? Can He do the impossible? At first glance, it appears that, however these questions are answered, God is unable to do everything, and not therefore not omnipotent. It would follow that God therefore couldn't be omnipotent, and that traditional theism is based upon a falsehood.

This problem is traditionally illustrated with the paradoxical question "Can God create a stone which is too heavy for him to lift up?" The thought here is that the answer must be either 'yes' or 'no'. But either way reveals a limitation on God's power. If the answer is 'yes', then there can be a stone too heavy for God to lift, so He is not omnipotent; if the answer is 'no' then there is a super heavy stone, which God cannot create, so He is not omnipotent. Since omnipotence is a defining characteristic of God, and we have just shown that the concept is self-contradictory, if follows that no being can be omnipotent, and hence that God does not exist.

The theist, however, has a range of possible replies. The first would be that this question does not pose a problem at all if God does not ever a) attempt to lift the stone or b) create an unliftable stone. If God were to simply avoid these two situations then he will be omnipotent for all time. However, given that this would result in the idea that God could destroy his own omnipotence and hence his divinity, whilst continuing to exist, it is hardly an ideal solution.

Another approach would be to say that God, particularly as the definition of free will, can freely choose to alter any laws that might hinder omnipotence. We can't understand how He would do this as humans we are limited in our worldview. But we could choose to trust that God is omnipotent and therefore able to do and conceive of things that we cannot on. Some view this explanation as ducking the problem; this is a really frustrating approach as it creates a God who we, as humans, cannot possibly comprehend. How then are theists meant to have a personal relationship with something so beyond comprehension? Faith becomes totally blind.

An alternative solution is to say that God cannot break the laws of logic. This does not imply that there is a realm of the do-able from which God is excluded – to say that something is logically impossible is precisely to exclude it from the realm of the do-able. If God cannot do what is logically impossible then it is not to say that his power is limited in any way. Following this logic, the theist can argue that it is not logically possible to pick up a stone that an omnipotent being has made unliftable. C.S. Lewis argued that referencing 'a rock so heavy that God cannot lift it' was as nonsensical as asking 'can God draw a square circle?' Following this argument the perceived paradox is meaningless.

Thomas Aquinas too argued that the paradox really arises from a misunderstanding of omnipotence. When one considers the meaning of omnipotence, the phrase 'could not lift' does not make sense, as he believed that God is able to do all things. He could part the Red Sea, save Daniel from the Lion's Den, and raise the dead. But those things do not defy logic.

Asking God to create something that would then create an impossible situation is not logical – so Aquinas would simply dismiss the question as nonsense.

Essentially this argument has shifted our understanding of omnipotence from 'a being who can do everything' to a 'being who can do everything which is logically possible.' This subsequently leaves us with a decision to make; what is more relevant to the concept of omnipotence – pure success? Or success and failure together?

One could question whether this change in definition is fair, but as it is the theists who are defending the claim that an omnipotent God exists, surely it is up to them to say what is meant their own belief. Some argue that omnipotence should really be redefined as 'almighty' or that God should simply not be referred to as omnipotent.

Even with this semantic deviance, an atheist could continue to attack the idea of omnipotence with the simple question 'Can God sin?' As God is by definition 'good' then surely he cannot sin. If he could then again, he would be able to destroy his divinity so that would not be a tenable solution. Is it logically impossible for an 'all good' being to not sin?

Whilst arguably, this is also a paradoxical question and one that can be avoid by simply dismissing it as such. We have found something that we as humans can do – but God cannot. If this is the case, then is He worthy of worship?

Omniscience

Jeremiah 29:11

For I know the plans I have for you," declares the LORD, "plans to prosper you and not to harm you, plans to give you hope and a future.

A further attribute applied to the God of traditional theism is that of omniscience – the state of knowing everything. In the previous section, the issue of what knowledge really entails was examined; for example, can God know what it is to have a headache if He does not have a corporal form? Whilst it was established this could be viewed as a paradoxical question, there are other issues that have to be examined.

Free will is the belief that humanity was 'gifted' with the ability to choose how we behave. No action or outcome is destined but rather, we make our own paths through virtue of our own decisions. 'Theological fatalism' contends that omniscience (or divine foreknowledge) and free will are incompatible, therefore any conception of God that incorporates both properties is inherently contradictory.

In theory, God knows all of our future actions, then the future is fixed. It follows that if the future is fixed, it seems that there is nothing that we can do to change it. If God knows that I have going to bring a packed lunch tomorrow, before tomorrow occurs, then do I have any choice in the matter? What it I want to go and scoff chips in the lunch hall? It seems that there is little choice in the matter if God already knows what I will do before I have carried out that action.

The ability to determine our future actions, though, is what constitutes human freedom. Divine foreknowledge, then, seems to preclude the possibility of our being free agents. So it seems, at first glance, that either we possess freewill, or God simply cannot be omniscient.

There are, of course, a number of answers. The first is to simply answer that we're not free. This appeals to logic in a number of ways, as so many of decisions in life are naturally determined by the events that preceded them. For example, whilst I could claim that I *chose* to go to University, I only really made that choice because of the thousands of chance occurrences that led to that decision - parental expectation, my schooling, the avoidance of real life... one could even say the circumstance of my birth. Given the idea of determinism exists outwit theism, the extension to say God is just one of these many determining factors isn't ridiculous... just rather depressing.

It also raises a number of problems from a Christian perspective: if humans do not possess freewill, then it would follow, that God has chosen some to have a relationship with him (and to be saved) whereas others were damned before they even began. For God's benevolence to be maintained, this option really needs to be rejected.

Another possible way round this problem is to suggest that God's perception of time is different from our own. As Calvin explained in Institutes of the Christian Religion:

When we attribute foreknowledge to God, we mean that all things have ever been, and perpetually remain, before His eyes, so that to His knowledge nothing is future or past, but all things are present: and present in such a manner that He does not merely conceive of them from ideas formed in His mind, as things remembered by us appear present to our minds, but really beholds and sees them as if actually placed before Him.

God, by existing outside and above the timeline, can view 'tomorrow' in the same way as we can view 'today.' For God all of time is 'Now'. He sees and knows things before you have experienced them because He is there now. You never suppose that your actions are less free because God knows what you are doing. In a way He does not know what you will do until you have done it: but then the moment at which you choose is already 'Now' for Him.

The idea of God being in all moments, is perhaps, a confusing one as we are very much stuck in the concept of time. However, we too have the benefit of being able to view the past; I know that I went to a restaurant and ate steak tonight, but I didn't have to, I could've chosen the chicken. It would be wrong to say that I HAD to eat steak just because I know that NOW. So what's the problem with saying that God knows what I will eat for breakfast tomorrow already? Traditional theism requires God to be omnipresent - in all places, at all times - so why not the future viewing all of those past decisions?

However, we once again are confronted with a number of criticisms: Can God then 'know' what it is like for time to pass, can He know what it is like to wait for tomorrow if each moment is now? If He cannot experience this knowledge can He truly be said to be omniscient? If He cannot know what it is like to be within time, can He really know individuals, and be with them throughout life? As Austin Cline writes, 'this, however, seems to reduce God to a type of computer storage bank: God contains all facts that exist, but nothing more interesting.'

A further option is to return to the point of paradox: one could fairly say that given I have not yet decided where to eat lunch tomorrow, it isn't logical to know where I will eat lunch, and therefore God isn't limited by not yet knowing. This isn't to say that He is lacking in any way, but rather that He knows all things He could know. But again, this really leads to a rather disappointing God: is there any point in praying to a being who doesn't know what the future holds? Or cannot change what is to happen?

An alternative approach to look at the belief that God created the universe – and everything in it. This means He created the possibility of physical activity, along with creating every experience possible. It is fair to believe that in His creation, He knows what He is creating. Therefore God knows the experience of swimming, and knows the taste of an apple, because it is He who created them. Even if we were to ignore the fact that God created every experience, and that we look at the claim that He cannot know certain experiences, Christians can always point to Jesus; as God incarnate it is possible to argue that God knows what it is to be limited in human form.

One could push against this point asking whether God could therefore know what it is like to be female – given Jesus' masculinity. But this could be further countered by the Christian belief that the Holy Spirit is in each of us. Indeed, as God is the creator of everything – His very essence is in each moment. These questions are asking him to be limited in a way that would make Him unworthy of worship or adoration, when in fact traditional theism renders Him far more than the sum of these things.

4 GOD AS DESIGNER

An alternative method of attack is to utilize modern science and attempt to find evidence that directly contradicts the beliefs of traditional theism. This is the favored starting point of the majority of New Atheists - as four out of the five leaders of this movement are leading scientists, this is perhaps unsurprising.

Theism tells us that God is a being who is omnipotent and omniscient, wholly self-sufficient, with no needs, or deficiencies of any kind. This being chose to create the universe and everything within it. This being apparently explains the complexity that we find in the universe e.g. the intricacies of the human eye or complex skeleton of the Venus' fly basket. Richard Swinburne highlighted the simplicity of this argument, in that it explained everything by invoking a single substance as creator and maintainer.

However, one must question whether we should follow Swinburne's logic at all. Is an entity that monitors and control every particle, that listens to our thoughts and prayers, who is imminent and transcendent, in time and out of time, really that simple? Surely this being would require a 'mammoth explanation' of its own. By Swinburne's own reasoning the theory of natural selection could be argued to be much simpler than the theory of the existence of such a complex being, and thus preferable. As Richard Dawkins writes,

> *The candidate solutions to the riddle of improbability are not, as is falsely implied, design and chance. They are design and natural selection. ... Natural selection is not only a parsimonious, plausible, and elegant; it is the only workable alternative to chance that has ever been suggested.*

In Climbing Mount Improbable, Dawkins expressed this point in a parable.

> *One side of the mountain is a sheer cliff, impossible to climb, but on the other side is a gentle slope to the summit. On the summit sits a complex device such as an eye or a bacterial flagellar motor. The absurd*

notion that such complexity could spontaneously self-assemble is symbolized by leaping from the foot of the cliff to the top in one bound. Evolution, by contrast, goes around the back of the mountain and creeps up the gentle slope to the summit: easy! The principle is so simple, one is tempted to marvel that it took so long for a Darwin to arrive on the scene and discover it.

The theist may highlight that Science does not explain everything. But it's here that we can apply to induction again. In the past things the unknown has turned out to have a naturalistic explanation. Surely it is reasonable to infer that this would continue to be the case?

So has the atheist disproved God with modern scientific findings? Certainly as an abductive argument it has its strengths. As Julian Baggini argued, it passes a number of criteria:

- Simple - We only need to posit the existence of natural world which is eminently testable
- Coherent - Everything fits into one scheme of being – no communication between 'realms'
- Comprehensive - Can explain all manner of things e.g. evil, diversity of religions, brain function without reliance on supernatural incomprehensible beings.

However, it should be noted once more that as an argument based on observation and experience it cannot be taken as a proof. Certainly, modern science can significantly reduce the probability that theism is true but cannot yet claim to have done much more than that.

On the contrary there are a number of theists who would argue on this point. A common criticism leveled at Dawkins is that he fundamentally has no real understanding of Christian beliefs, as Eagleton commented in his review of The God Delusion: 'Imagine someone holding forth on biology whose only knowledge of the subject is the Book of British Birds, and you have a rough idea of what it feels like to read Richard Dawkins on theology.'

Dawkins is under the misapprehension that the findings of modern science are completely incongruous with theism but for many this is simply not the case. As Stephen Jay Gould noted in Rock of Ages: 'Either half my colleagues are enormously stupid, or else the science of Darwinism is fully compatible with conventional religious beliefs – and equally compatible with atheism.'

Indeed, even the great stronghold of the Catholic Church has accepted Evolution as a theory. Writing in 1950, Pope Pius XII effectively set out to permit Catholics to believe the theory of evolution provided there is still room for the soul; Catholic doctrine dictates that God creates the soul and infuses it in each individual human; in his view these two theories can sit along side each other. Pope John Paul II reiterated this point in 1996 in his statement to the Pontifical Academy of Sciences. However he went further than his predecessor saying that there was so much evidence to support evolution that it was now beyond reasonable doubt and should not be denied, however he added the caveat:

The sciences of observation describe and measure the multiple manifestations of life with increasing precision and correlate them with the time line. The moment of transition to the spiritual cannot be the object of this kind of observation.

Sir Peter Medawar, an Oxford immunologist who won the Nobel Prize for medicine, made this point repeatedly. He explored the question of how science was limited by the nature of reality. Emphasizing that 'science is incomparably the most successful enterprise human beings have every engaged upon,' he distinguishes between what he calls 'transcendent' questions, which are better left to religion and metaphysics, and questions about the organization and structure of the material universe. This is encountered in Stephen Jay Gould's idea of the 'NOMA' (non-overlapping magisteria) of science and religion. The 'magisterium of science' deals with the 'empirical realm,' where as the 'magisterium of religion' deals with 'questions of ultimate meaning,' such as 'What are we all here for?' or 'What is the point of living?'

This idea particular enrages Dawkins who argues that if science cannot answer some ultimate question, what makes anybody think that religion can:

> *'... We have all been guilty of bending over backwards to be nice to an unworthy but powerful opponent... the presence or absence of a creative super-intelligence is unequivocally a scientific question, even if it is not in practice – or not yet – a decided one.'*

It is Dawkins view that that there is no place for theology in academic discussions and that religion has little to offer anyone. However, it does seem that Dawkins has a very narrow view of Christianity. For many, belief in God has nothing to do with creation or the existence of the universe. It is bad theology as well as bad science to imagine a 'God of the gaps' where God is invoked to explain anything that science can't. This is because God is not a 'thing' within the world that causes other 'things' to happen according to the normal observable physical laws of nature. God acts in a way that seems to obey a different set of laws, or operate in another dimension of reality that is not specifically accessible to scientific analysis or study, and which shows up in odd events in our own world. This could be discounted as nonsense, infantile beliefs just attempting to explain something that people cannot understand. However the problem for Dawkins is that religion really is not going anywhere. For billions of people worldwide the realm of Science does not offer enough answers, at least to the questions that they are asking.

Arguably, Dawkins insistence that Science is the only answer is providing the radical fundamentalist left-wing Christians with further ammunition; William Dembski, a leader of the Intelligent Designer movement (who wholly discount evolution) wrote that Dawkins work was 'God's greatest gift to the intelligent-design movement.'

Has Science rendered theism unlikely? It depends who you listen to. For many Science and theism are completely compatible and for all their rhetoric Dawkins and his fellow atheists have not yet convinced the world that religion has no place or even that

Science can explain away all of our questions. There is perhaps more weight found in further arguments.

5 SUFFERING AND EVIL

1 John 4:8

"Whoever does not love does not know God, because God is love."

The problem of evil suggests that traditional theism is incoherent with the way the world is. The world is full of evil and suffering; there are evil acts perpetrated by man, such as the murder of innocents, and there is also natural evil, the suffering caused by the mere operation of the laws of nature. Both the prevalence of crippling and agonizing diseases, and the huge cost in pain and distress caused by natural disasters, such as Earthquakes or Tsunamis, would both count as paradigms of natural evil. This would not only include the pain experienced by humans but also within the animal kingdom, most pointedly through natural selection itself. At first glance, this appears to be incongruent with the notion of the all-loving God. If God loves all people, is aware of suffering and has the power to do something about it then it is reasonable to suggest that He would act to put a stop to it.

The logical problem of evil emerges from the following **deductive** argument:

1. An all-powerful (omnipotent) God could prevent evil from existing in the world.
2. An all-knowing (omniscient) God would know that there was evil in the world.
3. An all-good (omnibenevolent) God would wish to prevent evil from existing in the world.
4. There is evil in the world therefore God does not exist.

Omnipotence, omniscience and omnibenevolence are all features of the Christian God, presented as *a priori* truths. However as the argument stands the theist must assert that at least one of the premises is false if he is to deny the truth of the conclusion. The easiest of these premises to tackle seems to be the third; surely it can be argued that an omnibenevolent God does not *necessarily* wish to prevent all evil?

An alternative approach would be to view God's goodness as different from our own. Rather than viewing God as impotent, or sadistic, one could posit that evil has a requirement and we shouldn't judge God by human standards of morality. But as Sam

Harris highlights in his Huffpost article, 'There Is No God (And You Know It)', "human standards of morality are precisely what the faithful use to establish God's goodness in the first place." So we are left with the question of whether the existence of evil and suffering could be viewed as the most moral solution – from human standards as well as the divine.

Religious Responses (Theodicies)

Note: Theodicy comes from the Greek: theos (God) and dike (justification) - is the name given to the attempt to demonstrate that there is no logical contradiction in supposing that God is all-loving, all-powerful and has a reason for allowing suffering and evil. In other words, it is still possible to believe in an almighty, loving God even though there is suffering in the world.

Augustinian Theodicy

Named for the 4th- and 5th-century theologian and philosopher Augustine of Hippo, the Augustinian Theodicy rests upon two significant beliefs: Firstly, whilst God created a perfect world, evil was brought into the Cosmos by the fall of angels after Lucifer chose to rebel against God. This was further compounded when Adam and Eve, tempted by the serpent, chose to disobey God. The key thing to note is that in both of these situations, the evil did not come from God, and He is therefore justified in allowing in to remain. Secondly, as evil has come from elsewhere, God is justified in allowing evil to remain.It's reasonable assume that Augustine viewed the Creation Account of Genesis as a literal version of events. It therefore follows that Augustine would've seen creation as fundamentally good given there various versions in Genesis 1 that state: "God saw all that he had made, and it was very good.' It would therefore be illogical to argue that evil was created by God in any way given it evidentially is not good. Augustine believe that evil was therefore a 'privation', or lack of something. Evil only occurs when a part of God's Creator Order does not act in the manner in which it was created. Augustine saw that Natural Evil is a result of humanity's rebellion – which upset this order – so a natural disaster can be viewed as a punishment for this sin. If God were to stop this suffering, he wouldn't be just. Whilst one could question why 'innocent' individual's have to suffer in such events, Augustine's answer is simple: all of us are guilty as descendants of Adam and Eve.

However, all hope is not lost as Augustine does highlight God's grace: Jesus Christ, through His redeeming sacrifice on the cross, gave Humans the opportunity to make amends through a rejection of evil, and turning back to Christ. As stated in John 3:17, 'For God did not send his Son into the world to condemn the world, but to save the world through him.' Jesus' death atones for the sins of humanity through all time, freely choosing to give humanity a chance to avoid the punishment of Hell. It follows that at the end of time, we will all be judged, and those who have chosen to accept Jesus' sacrifice will be saved – showing both God's merciful and just nature.

On the contrary, the Augustinian Theodicy can be found to fail as an adequate defence on a number of points. Firstly, if God created a 'perfect' world, how could it go wrong? If God is truly omniscience then He surely knew that mankind would 'fall' – yet He continued with His design. The acceptance that Hell exists indicates that God designed the world knowing that He would later punish His creation; this seems far from just.

The classic Christian response to this argument is to focus on free will: if Adam and Eve hadn't had the possibility of disobedience, any relationship with God would have would have then been forced. Love can only be possible in a situation of total freedom - there can be no compulsion. A world populated by people compelled to love God, or to act in a moral way, would in fact be non-moral. One could question whether this is the best possible world, as whilst mere humans cannot conceive of an alternative that allows both freedom and no evil, surely an omnipotent God would be able to create something better than this?

A further problem of Augustine's theory is obviously that it rests upon a literal interpretation of the biblical account. Modern Creation theories such as Evolution raises a number of issues for this: Natural evil existed longer before there were humans to punish, and by the same token, the moral evil entering the world in the Garden of Eden, appears to have no place in our current world view.

One could argue that Augustine could be viewed in mythological terms – focusing on a myth to give understanding to spiritual truth. It cannot be ignored that for all of humanity to have freewill – choice – there has to be something to choose between e.g. good and evil. However, many would point out that for a 'privation', evil is a very powerful experience and given that one can choose to increase it – it must be seen as an entity in it's own right.

Irenaean Theodicy

The Irenaean theodicy is named after Second-century philosopher and theologian Irenaeus, who proposed a two-stage creation process in which humans require free will and the experience of evil to develop. It is sometimes referred to as the 'soul making theodicy', as according to the Irenaean tradition, God did not create mankind to be automatically perfect, but rather with the ability to reach perfection. It builds upon the point that we found in relation to the Augustinian theodicy – that to truly have freewill one must have something to freely choose between. Both good and evil must exist in opposition to each other, in order for us to have something to choose between. It is only then that we can really develop moral virtue; this duality must exist through all of nature, or else would be an artificial construct, and therefore explains both moral and natural suffering and evil.

Irenaeus proposed, that whilst Humans were created in the image of God, they were not created in His likeness. Humans can only become *like* God if they freely chose can act co-operatively with Him. Throughout our lives we change from being human animals to "children of God". This is a choice made after struggle and experience as we choose God rather than our baser instincts. Suffering and evil don't exist to our detriment but rather because it gives Humans the opportunity to become like God. It follows that Evil needs to exist and not be stopped for a number of reasons: firstly the world needs to act in a way that is predictable so that we may learn from it – if evil sometimes resulted in happiness rather we would be unable to acquire knowledge, e.g. hunger leads to pain, so we eat to avoid it. Secondly, if we were programmed to do the right thing, or faced punishment immediately for wrong doing then it would be impossible to build character – or eventually achieve godlike perfection.

However, one must question whether this argument really is sufficient to justify evil? Firstly, many people claim to be moral beings without ever experiencing any real level of suffering and those who have suffered often have become dehumanised and become more evil as a consequence. Is there honestly any conceivable good which could only be achieved by the occurrence of (say) millions of people being tortured and killed, and which is so great that it would somehow counterbalance all that suffering? Secondly, one could question what possible benefit the death of an infant bring could bring – they are surely equally human yet have no chance to morally develop through that experience. Does the suffering of a baby really justify the development of another? Furthermore, suffering seems to be entirely disproportionate to this benefit - is natural evil on such a mass scale like earthquakes and tsunamis really necessary for the formation of moral virtue? The Irenaean theodicy asserts that the world is the best of all possible worlds because it allows humans to fully develop, but surely, an all-loving, all-powerful God could have conceived of a better system? It seems that the world contains a great deal more evil, both moral and natural, that it needs to.

John Hick, in his development of Irenaeus' Theodicy goes someway in addressing these issues. He makes the point, that evil does have to actually be bad – if it wasn't then there would be no real compulsion to follow God's law. If evil was akin to receiving a Lunchtime Detention it would be possible to shrug off. Hick makes the point, that the world isn't paradise – it's not meant to be – it's intended to give us the opportunity to become morally excellent individuals; something he refers to as 'soul-making'. Whilst, suffering doesn't always look like it results in human development, Hick highlights that life does not end with death. Whilst many people appear to suffer as victims of this system, it's reasonable to assume that God would not punish them for this and they would have their place in heaven. Indeed, Irenaeus held the view that everyone will go to Heaven – regardless of their performance on Earth.

However, this seems unfair on a number of counts: why is it that some people are tested more than others? If everyone gets to go to Heaven then this seems rather unjust. This also directly contradicts the teaching of the Bible which promises that the righteous will have their place in Heaven. It also seems to remove the motivation for trying: if I got paid regardless of whether I went to work or not, you would most certainly find me lounging in a coffee shop rather than marking essays or writing reports!

Additionally, whilst Hick's point that 'evil needs to be evil' is fairly compelling, did we really need as many disasters to occur as we've seen? Could the Rwandan Genocide not have lasted 50 days instead of 100? Could Hurricane Katrina not have been a Category 4 instead? Richard Swinburne attempts to defend this point by arguing that if God were to scale back this atrocities, He would in turn be scaling back human freedom. If we didn't have the option to commit Genocide rather than individual murder then would that be true freedom? However, one must question, is this truly love? Is the hurt in the world really an expression of the love of the Divine? Swinburne makes the point, that a good parent punishes their child if they misbehave, slowly allowing them greater freedom as they grow. But one could question whether this is a good analogy given that the 'naughty step' is rather different from the existence of malaria!

6 THE IMPROBABILITY OF GOD

It should be obvious that atheists propose that the existence of God is highly improbable. Of course, the flip side to this is that theists propose that the existence of God is, in fact, probable. Whilst there are modern writers, such as Stephen Unwin, who developed a mathematical theory to conclude that the probably of God existing is 67 percent. It would be fairer to say that the founder of probability theory, in relation to theism, is actually French mathematician and physicist Blaise Pascal.

Having come to a personal faith in Christ at the age of thirty-one, Pascal had planned to write his own defence of the Christian faith, but he died with his notes unpublished at the age of only thirty-nine years. Fortunately, his notes were published posthumously as the *Pensees.* Pascal maintained that life was utterly futile without God, and even if you're too much of an ignoramus to see the signs in nature, he argued that probability was on the side of God. It for this 'wager' that he is remembered: Pascal argued that life is a game already in progress, so a bet must be laid. There is no avoiding it as you have been born into the game. You have two options — God exists or He doesn't. Pascal argued that given the odds are even, it is reasonable to choose either option. But he points out that if one wagers that God does exist, one gains eternal life in heaven. If it turns out He doesn't, then one has lost nothing. If one wagers that God doesn't exist, and then He does, then all one gains is eternity in Hell. But if you have wagered correctly, you gain nothing but the knowledge that you were right. Hence, he argued, the most prudent choice is to believe that God does exist.

The obvious response to this is to question whether the odds really are that even to begin with. Is it really fair to say that God is a plausible option given the incoherence of His attributes? When individual qualities are examined, such as omnipotence, it's possible to argue for a redefinition or that a misunderstanding has occurred. But when traits are seen in combination, such as omnipotence and omniscience, problems emerge e.g. God could surely never know what it is like to be unable to do something. We've found that in defending one criticism, another criticism in turn against weight. Whilst it is logical for God to be able to do anything, that in turn limits His knowledge. The result is a God who is very different from the one proposed by traditional theism.

Further to this, one could also ponder whether it's really as simple as Pascal makes out. The 'game of life' isn't a two horse race of Atheism or Theism – should Allah, Zeus, Thor, Durga, and every other god and goddess not be included? How should they be factored into this wager?

Is there any harm in being theist?

One only has to see the chapter headings of *The God Delusion* to find Dawkin's answer to this question; 'Childhood, abuse and the escape from religion' leaves little to the imagination. Similarly entitled books such as Dennett's *Breaking the Spell: Religion as a Natural Phenomenon* or Hitchen's *God is Not Great: How Religion Poisons Everything* give further indication as to the New Atheist's opinion on the topic. Sam Harris' *Letter to a Christian Nation* is an eloquent treatise on the myths of which he believes Christianity was built and the inherent danger of religion, he writes:

> *Clearly, it is time we learned to meet our emotional needs without embracing the preposterous. We must find ways to invoke the power of ritual and to mark those transitions in every human life that demand profundity – birth, marriage, death – without lying to*

ourselves about the nature of reality... only then will we stand a chance of healing the deepest and most dangerous fractures in our world.

These 'dangerous fractures' can most clearly be seen in the actions done in the name of God. Whether it's small scale violence, patriarchal oppression, systematic abuse or the bloody crusades, murderous inquisitions, or corrupt governments irradiating minority groups – there is no doubt that religion has increased the suffering and evil in the world rather than decrease it in anyway.

It can of course be argued that these are acts of madmen, and an indication of the fallen humanity, rather than wished for by God. If people did not fight in the name of God, or turn to extremism using religion as an excuse, they would simply find something else. Humans are by nature really quite violent. However, the point stands that religion is unique in that it is the only form of in-group/out-group thinking that casts the differences between people in terms of eternal rewards.

What about those who argue that Christ had some worthy teaching such as preaching against violence, or giving up material possessions? Arguably you find very few Christians who actually follow such teachings. Besides which, Christ also taught that anyone who disregarded his message would face eternal damnation. As Bertrand Russell wrote: 'You do not, for instance find that attitude in Socrates. You find him quite bland and urbane toward the people who would not listen to him; and it is, to my mind, far more worthy of sage to take that line than to take the line of indignation.'

Is there a solution?

We must accept that, as Christian theology has always claimed that faith does not emerge from a process of argument and it seems the same is true for disbelief. Faith can be aided by careful thinking but for the majority it emerges when a person believes they have encountered God themselves at a much deeper level than the merely rational. Therefore, whilst arguments against the existence of God may push the believer to question the logic of their belief, as the New Atheist movement has shown, they have not exactly forced the believers into submission. All in all, at times it simply seems to strengthen their convictions.

In Britain, certainly since 1689 we have been tolerant of belief, allowing people to believe what they will, whilst recognising there right to do so. That is not to say discussion between those with faith, and those with none is not fruitful or healthy. Both theists and atheists have recognised a need for society to become more 'moral' and for there to be a set of workable morals for all to follow. Our legal system remains free of religious bias for this very reason. It seems the responsibility of all those who wish to shape society to continue to make their voices heard. Above all, given all this uncertainty, perhaps it is just easier to highlight the absence of certainty in either direction and just get on with living.

ABOUT THE AUTHOR

Laura Crichton is a teacher of Religious, Moral, and Philosophical Studies at Stewart's Melville College, Edinburgh. She gained her degree in Divinity at the University of Aberdeen, before completing teacher training at the University of Edinburgh. She has taught Advanced Higher RMPS since 2009 and is a marker for the Scottish Qualifications Authority - at both Higher and Advanced Higher.

Printed in Great Britain
by Amazon

71793742R00040